Illustrator:
Barb Lorseyedi

Editor:
Janet Cain, M. Ed.

Editorial Project Manager:
Ina Massler Levin, M.A.

Editor in Chief:
Sharon Coan, M.S. Ed.

Art Director:
Elayne Roberts

Associate Designer:
Denise Bauer

Cover Artist:
Larry Bauer

Production Manager:
Phil Garcia

Imaging:
Alfred Lau

Publishers:
Rachelle Cracchiolo, M.S. Ed.
Mary Dupuy Smith, M.S. Ed.

January
Monthly Activities

Early Childhood

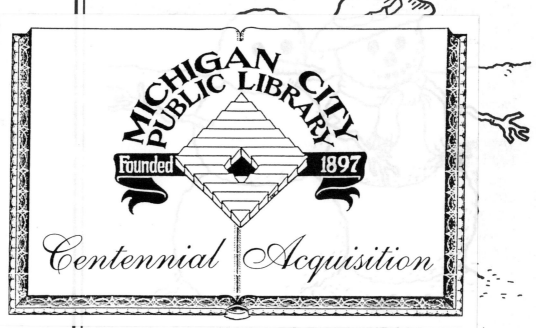

Author:
Dona Herweck Rice

Teacher
Created
Materials

Teacher Created Materials, Inc.
P.O. Box 1040
Huntington Beach, CA 92647
©*1996 Teacher Created Materials, Inc.*
Made in U.S.A.
ISBN-1-55734-864-2

Table of Contents

Introduction

The monthly activity books in this series have been created specifically for early childhood students. Every book is divided into four themes, roughly one theme per week of the month. Within each weekly theme, there is a lesson-planning sheet; a parent sign in/out sheet; a list of suggested home activities; a number of thematic activities, such as arts and crafts, stories, letters, numbers, colors, shapes, music, movement, and food; a just for fun page; an original poem; stationery; clip art and patterns; bookmarks and badges for rewards; and an award certificate for one area of achievement. A calendar pattern, to which each student can add dates and a picture, and a request letter are included for the entire month. The themes for the month of January are *birthdays, homes, hats and mittens,* and *bears*. A variety of management materials have been included to support each theme, creating a unifying whole.

All activities are designed to enhance motor and/or cognitive skills while students are having fun. Most importantly, the activities have been classroom tested—with excellent results. Use some or all of the pages to support the already exciting early childhood experience taking place in your classroom.

January Calendar

Sunday	Monday	Tuesday	Wednesday	Thursday	Friday	Saturday

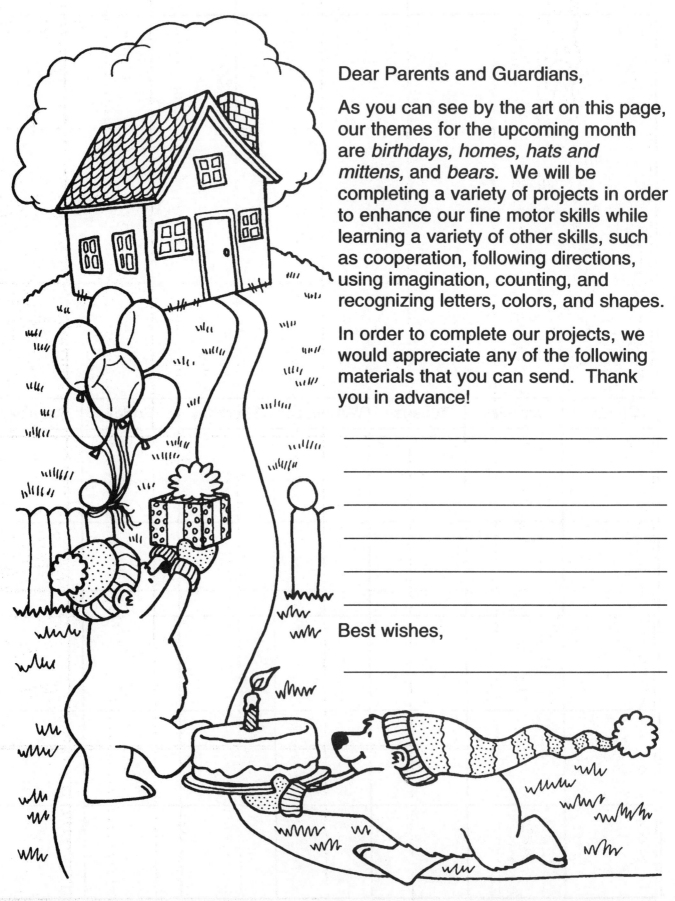

Dear Parents and Guardians,

As you can see by the art on this page, our themes for the upcoming month are *birthdays, homes, hats and mittens,* and *bears.* We will be completing a variety of projects in order to enhance our fine motor skills while learning a variety of other skills, such as cooperation, following directions, using imagination, counting, and recognizing letters, colors, and shapes.

In order to complete our projects, we would appreciate any of the following materials that you can send. Thank you in advance!

_____

_____

_____

_____

_____

Best wishes,

_____

Activity (circle time, playtime, etc.)	Monday	Tuesday	Wednesday	Thursday	Friday

Parent Sign In/Out Sheet

Parents: Please sign your child in and
out under the current date.

Name	Time	Date:	Date:	Date:	Date:	Date:
	In					
	Out					
	In					
	Out					
	In					
	Out					
	In					
	Out					
	In					
	Out					
	In					
	Out					
	In					
	Out					
	In					
	Out					
	In					
	Out					
	In					
	Out					

Birthday Activities for Home

Dear Parents and Guardians,

Our theme of the week is *birthdays*. Below is a list of enjoyable activities that you can do with your child. Please use some or all of these activities to support your child's learning. Your help is greatly appreciated.

Suggested Activities:

- Tell your child the story of his or her birth. Also tell your child the story of your birth.

- Discuss the birth of the new year.

- Make a birthday crown or cake just for fun. You can choose something unusual to celebrate, such as the birth of Tuesday or the 1,550th day of your child's life. You can also celebrate an "unbirthday," as in *Alice's Adventures in Wonderland* (Live Home Video, 1973).

- From your local library and with your child, check out a birthday storybook or nonfiction book. Read it together. Discuss your favorite parts with one another.

- Tell your child the story of a memorable birthday that you had when you were a child. Share any family photographs or home movies of past birthday celebrations, especially of your child's birthdays that he or she does not remember.

- Each of you can draw and color a picture of something related to birthdays, such as a birthday party, cake, or present. Tell about your pictures.

- Teach your child how to wrap a present.

- Show your child how to inflate a balloon, although the task itself is likely to be too difficult for him or her.

- Together, watch a birthday video for children, such as *Barney's Birthday* (The Lyons Group, 1992), *Winnie the Pooh, Vol. 4: Day for Eyeore* (Disney Home Video, 1983), or *The Busy World of Richard Scarry: The Best Birthday Present Ever* (PolyGram Video, 1993). After viewing the video, discuss it. Each of you can tell about your favorite parts.

- Go to a local party supply store to look at all the party favors.

- Read "Celebrate" with your child.

Best wishes,

_____

Birthday Arts and Crafts

The most important birthday to each person is, of course, the day on which he or she is born. To celebrate the birth of each student, make a class baby book. Here is how.

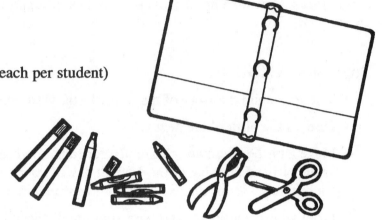

Materials:

- cover pattern (page 9)
- inside pages (pages 10 and 11, one of each per student)
- white index paper
- crayons and/or markers
- scissors
- hole punch
- three binder rings

Directions:

1. Reproduce pages 10 and 11 for students. Have them take page 11 home to complete with their parents. They should bring their papers back to school the next day.

2. Have students complete page 10. They can color pictures of themselves as newborns. Help each student write his or her name on the line.

3. Have each student also color the borders on pages 10 and 11.

4. Color or let students color the cover page (page 9). Invite them to write their names on the cover, as well.

5. Stack the pages, putting each student's two pages together and placing the cover on top of the stack.

6. Punch three holes down the left margin of the stack. Insert the three binder rings.

7. Share your classroom baby book at an Open House, Back-to-School Night, or another activity involving students and their parents.

8. A reward badge for this activity can be found on page 22.

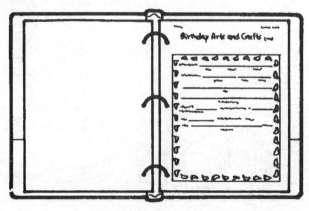

Birthday Arts and Crafts *(cont.)*

Our Classroom Baby Book

by_____

_____

_____

_____

_____

_____

_____

Birthday Arts and Crafts *(cont.)*

Draw a picture of yourself as you looked on the day you were born—your real BIRTHday!

Name _____

Birthday Arts and Crafts *(cont.)*

My name is

_____.
first   middle   last

I was born on

_____ _____, _____.
month   day   year

in

_____,
city

_____.
state or country

I weighed

_____ pounds/kilograms and _____ ounces/grams.

I was

_____ inches/centimeters long.

I was a _____ baby!
adjective

Birthday Letters

Practice the letter **Y** for *year.* Tell students that their ages say how many years they have lived. Point out that each year is counted with their birthdays. Have students color in the giant letters on this page. Ask them to draw birthday hats on the Y's.

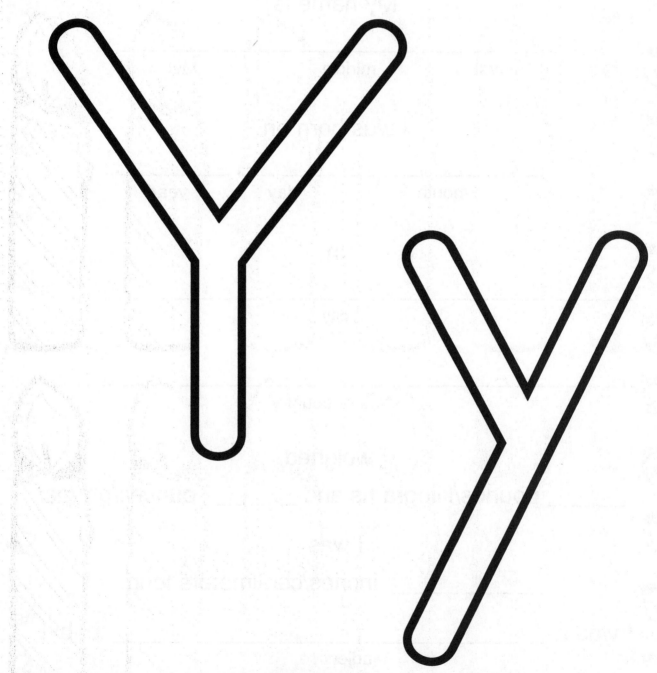

A reward badge for this activity can be found on page 22.

Birthday Numbers

Give each student a pile of birthday candles. If you prefer to use real candles rather than the patterns provided below, send a note home on the birthday stationery (page 19), asking parents to send one or two boxes of birthday candles. Call out an age and have students count out the corresponding number of candles. If desired, students can place their candles on the cake pattern (page 20). As students develop their counting skills, have "birthday-candle races" by allowing individuals or teams to compete as they count.

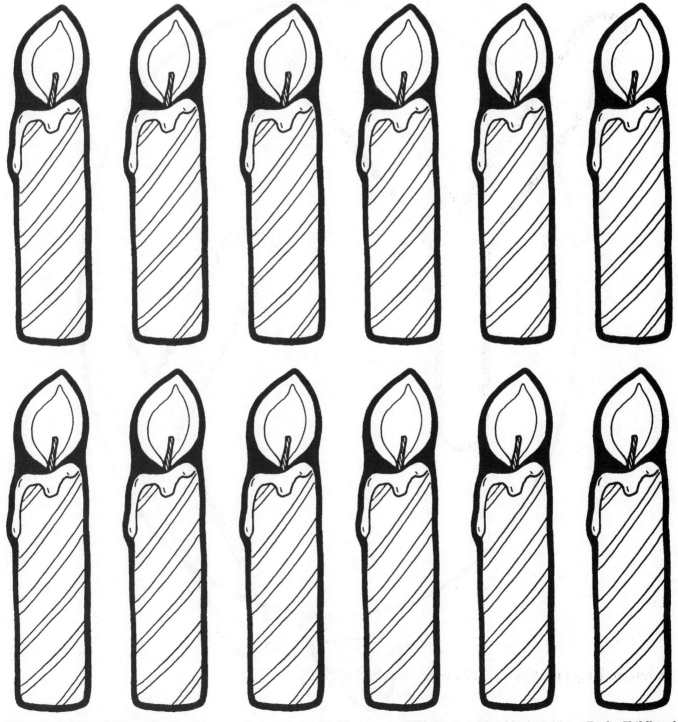

Birthday Shapes

Use your finger to trace the oval shown below, excluding the knotted end at the bottom. Together, name this basic shape. Reproduce the balloon pattern for students. Have each student cut out two patterns. Have students hold their two patterns together as you punch holes around the edges that are spaced about two inches (5 cm) apart. Let students use yarn to stitch the two ovals about three-quarters of the way around. Then they can stuff the ovals with crumpled newspaper and complete the stitching. Tie a length of yarn to the bottom of each balloon shape at the knot and suspend the birthday balloons from the ceiling.

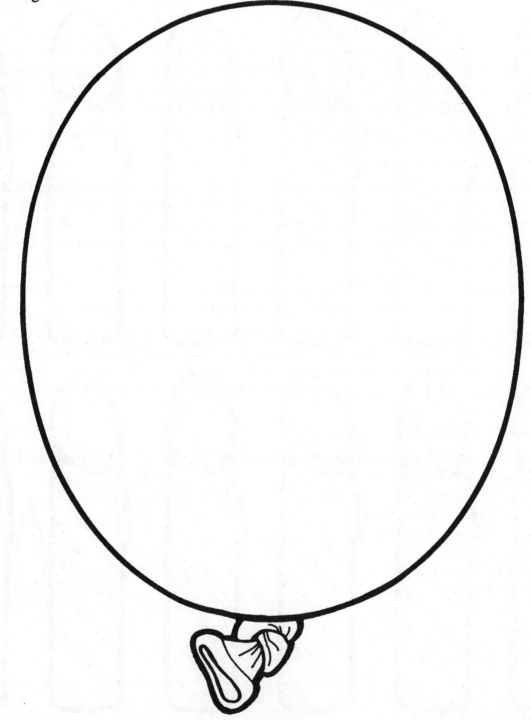

Birthday Music and Movement

This activity incorporates a variety of skills, and it will be a great deal of fun for students.

Materials:

- wrapped boxes (one per student)
- picture instruction cards (page 16)
- party hats (one per student)
- birthday or festive music

Directions:

1. Prepare the wrapped packages and party hats ahead of time. Place one picture instruction card (page 16) inside each box. Wrap the boxes in a variety of solid-colored paper. (**Note:** You may wish to solicit the help of older students or parent volunteers to do the wrapping.) Then make the party hats according to the directions provided at the bottom of this page.

2. Have students stand in a circle. Let them wear their party hats. Sing "Happy Birthday" together.

3. Give each student a wrapped package.

4. Play some festive music, such as "Somebody's Birthday" from *Greg and Steve: Holidays and Special Times* (Chameleon Records, 1989), "Shake My Sillies Out" from several of Raffi's records (Troubadour Records), or any number of songs from Nancy and John Cassidy's *Kids Songs: A Holler-Along Handbook* (Klutz Press, 1986) or *Kids Songs Two: Another Holler Along Handbook* (Klutz Press, 1988).

5. While the music plays, have students pass the packages around the circle. At an arbitrary time, stop the music and ask each student to name the color of his or her package.

6. Repeat Step 5 several times. Then have each student open the package he or she is holding. You may wish to have all of the packages opened at the same time or have students open them one at a time. Tell students to follow the directions on the picture instruction cards inside their packages. Remind students to follow all safety rules when participating in the movement part of this activity.

Directions for Party Hats:

Roll cone-shaped party hats out of large pieces of construction paper. Tape or staple each hat along the seam. Fold the hats so that the cones lay flat. Trim any excess paper along the bottoms. Help students identify the shape of the hats. Encourage them to decorate their hats with crayons, markers, sequins, fabric scraps, pompons, etc. Attach a length of string or yarn to opposite sides of each hat. Use the strings or yarn to tie the hats under the students' chins.

Birthday Music and Movement *(cont.)*

Reproduce the picture instruction cards for use with the activity described on page 15. Delete any movements that are too difficult for your students.

Hop on one foot.

Hop on two feet.

Spin in a circle.

Do a somersault.

Walk in a straight line.

Walk backwards.

The Birthday Gift

Connect the dots to find the special birthday present. Color the picture.

Celebrate

Kick up your heels and shout, "Hooray!"
A celebration's on the way!
Blow a whistle, throw confetti,
Hoot 'n holler 'til you're ready.
Clap your hands and then stomp your feet.
Be prepared for a super treat.
Jingle some bells and hang balloons.
The band will start to play a tune.
This is a very special day.
You're just in time for _____'s
birthday!

Note: Help each student fill in his or her own name.

Clip Art and Patterns

Note: Candle patterns can be found on pages 13 and 21.

Clip Art and Patterns *(cont.)*

Bookmarks and Badges

I am
_____

years old.

I know
the letter
Y.

Have each student write in his or her
age and then draw the correct number
of candles on the cake. Students can
color their badges and wear them home.

Have students color their badges and
wear them home.

My
birthday
is on
_____

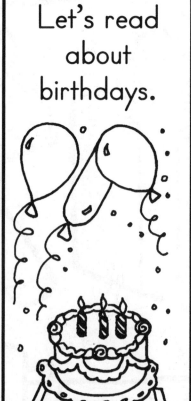
Let's read
about
birthdays.

Happy
Birthday!

Help each student fill in the month and
day of his or her birthday. Have
students color the badges and then wear
them home.

Although most early childhood students
have not yet learned to read, they enjoy
having bookmarks to use while reading
with their families at home.

Achievement Award

_____

has earned our

Classroom Achievement Award

for

NEATNESS!

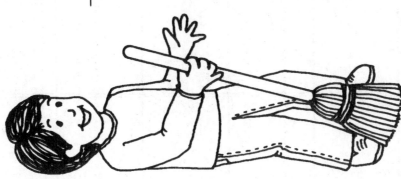

_____
Teacher's Signature

_____
Date

Activity (circle time, playtime, etc.)	Monday	Tuesday	Wednesday	Thursday	Friday

Parent Sign In/Out Sheet

Parents: Please sign your child in and out under the current date.

Name	Time	Date:	Date:	Date:	Date:	Date:
	In					
	Out					
	In					
	Out					
	In					
	Out					
	In					
	Out					
	In					
	Out					
	In					
	Out					
	In					
	Out					
	In					
	Out					
	In					
	Out					
	In					
	Out					

Homes Activities for Home

Dear Parents and Guardians,

Our theme of the week is *homes*. Below is a list of enjoyable activities that you can do with your child. Please use some or all of these activities to support your child's learning. Your help is greatly appreciated.

Suggested Activities:

- Ask your child to name his or her favorite things about home.

- Tell your child some of your favorite things about your current home. You might also wish to share what you think was special about a home you had as a child.

- If your child does not already know your phone number and address, teach this important information to him or her.

- Ask your child to name different kinds of animal homes. Take a walk in your community or a nearby park and look for animal homes in nature.

- When driving or walking down the street, talk with your child about the different kinds of homes the two of you see.

- Take your child to the public library. Check out a storybook or nonfiction book about homes for people or animals. Read it together. Discuss your favorite parts with one another.

- Each of you can draw and color a picture of a dream home. The size, style, special features, and location of your dream homes can be anything you desire. Tell about your pictures.

- Look through model homes with your child.

- Discuss the different kinds of homes people live in throughout the world. Then talk about how homes have changed throughout history.

- Use your imaginations to consider what homes on other planets might be like.

- Put together an ant farm. Observe the ants and discuss their habits.

- Read "Homes" with your child. Draw illustrations with your child of some of the homes named. Rewrite the poem, filling in the names and homes of family members. Examples: Grandma lives inside a house; Uncle Don lives in an apartment. (Do not worry about whether the lines rhyme.)

- Together, list all the things you can that have to do with homes.

Best wishes,

_____

Homes Arts and Crafts

Give each student a copy of the home pattern shown below and on page 28. Prepare the patterns as follows: Cut the door and windows along the dotted lines. Place the two pattern pieces together back to back. Fold the tabs and glue them on to the roof. Slide an 11" x 17" (27.5 cm x 42.5 cm) sheet of construction paper between the two pattern pieces just under the roof. Glue the construction paper in place, making sure not to glue down the door or windows. Then have each student color the house and background, draw his or her family behind the door and windows, and write his or her last name on the front of the house.

Homes Arts and Crafts *(cont.)*

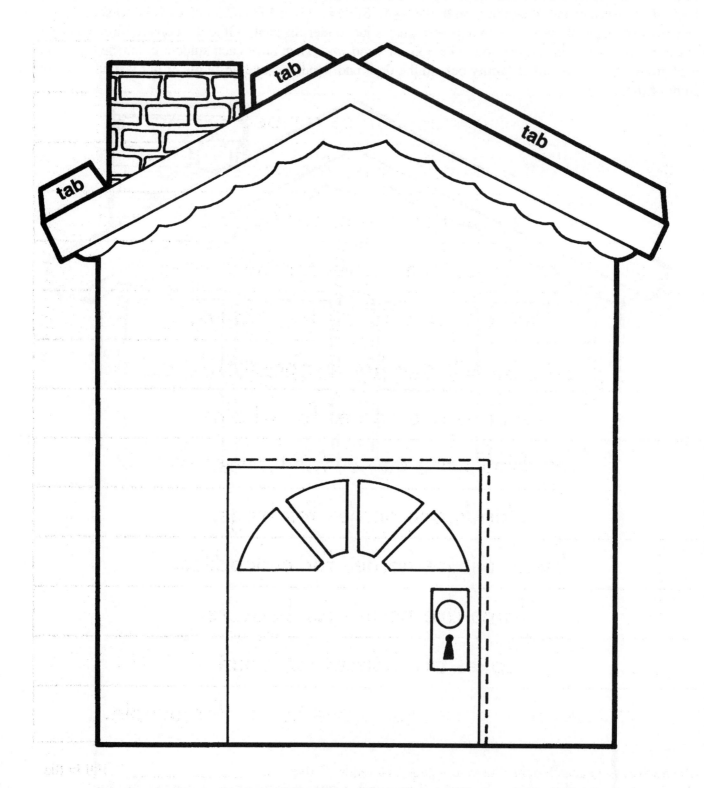

Homes Story

Cut apart the sentence strips shown below. Glue each sentence strip to the bottom of a sheet of paper. Let each student illustrate one sentence. Make a cover sheet with students' names on it as authors. Bind the book according to the directions on page 8.

Nests are homes for birds.
Caves are homes for bears.
Dens are homes for wolves.
Hives are homes for bees.
Trees are homes for owls.
Burrows are homes for rabbits.
Anthills are homes for ants.
Oceans are homes for whales.
Shells are homes for turtles.
Ponds are homes for frogs.
Swamps are homes for crocodiles.
Dams are homes for beavers.
Lakes are homes for trout.
Houses and apartments are homes for people.

Alternative: Let each student illustrate a page that reads, "I live in a _____." **Fill in the** blank for each student.

Homes Letters

Practice the letter **L** for *love*, the most important thing in a home. Have students color in the giant letters on this page, decorating them with hearts. Tell them that now they have written their first love "letters." Encourage students to deliver the "letters" to their parents.

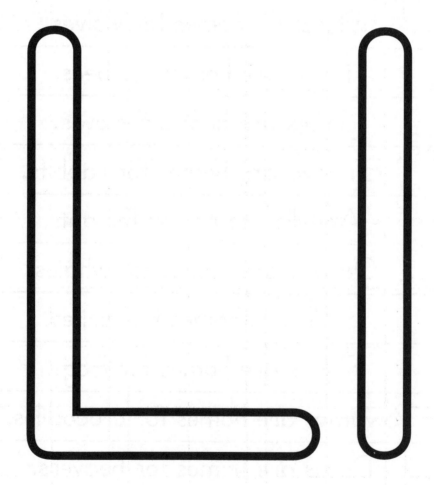

A reward badge for this activity can be found on page 41.

Homes Numbers

How many windows are in your home? Color a window on this page for every window in your home. Write the number of windows on the line. _____

Alternative 1: Instead of sending this paper home, count the windows in your classroom or school.

Alternative 2: Cut out a number of felt squares and rectangles and tell students they are windows. Have students pretend that your flannel board is a house. Place several windows on the board and ask students to count how many windows there are in the house. Take them down and repeat with a different number of windows.

Homes Colors

Let each student make a box look like his or her home by following these steps.

Materials:

- cardboard boxes (one per student)
  Square and rectangular facial tissue boxes work well.
- white wrapping or butcher paper
- scissors
- clear tape
- tempera paints (variety of colors)
- Styrofoam bowls
- paintbrushes
- cardboard or index paper scraps
- crayons
- smocks (one per student)
- tagboard (optional)

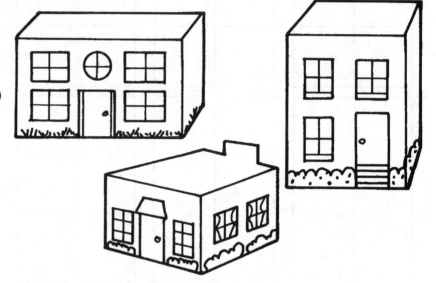

Directions:

1. Inform parents ahead of time of the date for this project since it will be a messy day. You can send notes to parents on the homes stationery (page 38), asking them to send old shirts or smocks if you do not already have some.

2. Wrap each box in white paper. **Note:** You may wish to solicit the help of older students or parent volunteers to help with the wrapping.

3. Have each student choose a box. Encourage students to select boxes that remind them of the shapes of their homes.

4. Give each student a smock. Ask each to choose a color of paint that is similar to the outside of his or her home. Say the name of each chosen color aloud. Then let students paint their boxes. Allow the paint to dry.

5. Let students use black paint to add windows and doors. Cut items, such as chimneys and balconies, from cardboard or index paper for students. Help glue these in place.

6. If desired, have students organize their painted homes into a community by gluing them in rows on a large piece of tagboard. Help students color trees, fences, and other items on pieces of cardboard or index paper and then glue them in place on the tagboard. Each student can make a sign to go in front of his or her house that reads, "_____'s House."

Homes Shapes

Help students identify each of the shapes shown below. Either give each student a set of these shapes cut from index paper to glue together or from felt to use on a flannel board. Let each student make a house from the shapes.

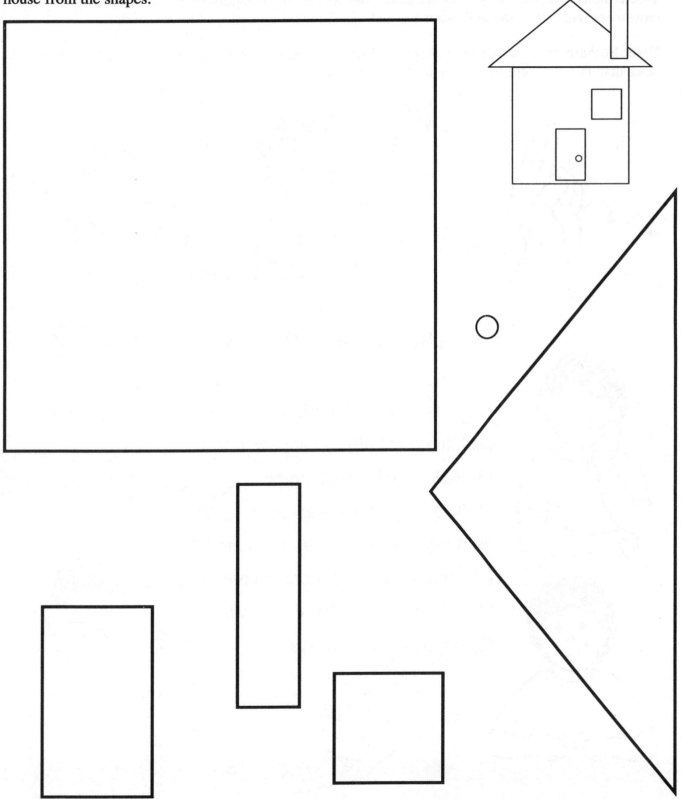

Homes Music and Movement

This is a folk song and hand-play activity. Demonstrate it for students. When they are very familiar with it, have them omit one line at a time, doing only the hand movements without the words. (This is done in much the same way you omit letters and only do the clapping when singing "Bingo.") The movements are shown in the illustrations and match the lines numbered in the poem.

Note: Because this is a folk song, there are different variations in existence. If you know a version other than this one, feel free to use it with your students.

Little Cabin in the Woods

(1) Little cabin in the woods,

(2) Little boy (girl) by window stood.

(3) Saw a rabbit hopping by,

(4) Knocking at his (her) door.

(5) "Help me! Help me! Help me!" it said,

(6) "Before the hunter shoots me dead!"

(7) "Come, little rabbit, come with me.

(8) Happy we will always be."

Homes Food

Bread was once the most traditional homemade food. You may wish to ask parent volunteers to send loaves of homemade bread for students to sample. Then let students have the opportunity to **bake bread** by following the recipe shown below. It yields one small loaf. Make one loaf for every four **students.** Enjoy the homemade bread with fresh-squeezed orange juice or lemonade.

Note: Ask parents if their children have any food allergies or dietary restrictions.

Ingredients:

- 3 cups (750 mL) all-purpose flour
- 1 tablespoon (15 mL) sugar
- ½ cup (125 mL) water
- 1 tablespoon (15 mL) butter

- 1 package quick-acting active dry yeast
- 1 teaspoon (5 mL) salt
- ⅓ cup (83 mL) milk
- 1 egg

Materials:

- large bowl
- saucepan
- cutting board or clean counter top
- greased cookie sheet
- oven mitt

- wooden spoon
- stove
- clean and dry kitchen towel
- oven

Preparation:

1. Mix the yeast, sugar, salt, and half the flour in the bowl.
2. Use a saucepan to heat the water, milk, and butter until they are very warm but not hot.
3. Carefully stir the water mixture into the flour mixture.
4. Stir in the egg.
5. Mix in enough of the remaining flour to make the dough easy to handle.
6. Sprinkle the cutting board or counter with flour. Knead the dough on the floured surface for about five minutes or until it is smooth and elastic.
7. Cover the dough with the towel and let it sit for ten minutes.
8. Shape the dough into a round or oval loaf. Place it on the greased cookie sheet. Cover it with the towel once more and let it rise for another 20 minutes. Meanwhile, heat the oven to 400° F (200° C).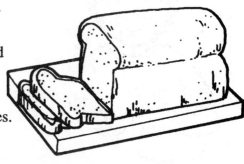
9. Bake the loaf until it is golden brown, about 20 to 25 minutes.
10. Serve warm, either plain or with butter and jam.

Whose Home Is It?

Draw lines to match everybody to his or her home.

Homes

Chipmunks live inside the trees.

Honey hives are for the bees.

Beavers live inside their dams.

Barns are good for baby lambs.

Burrows are a place for mice.

Lions think their caves are nice.

Dolphins live within the sea,

My home is just right for me.

38

Clip Art and Patterns

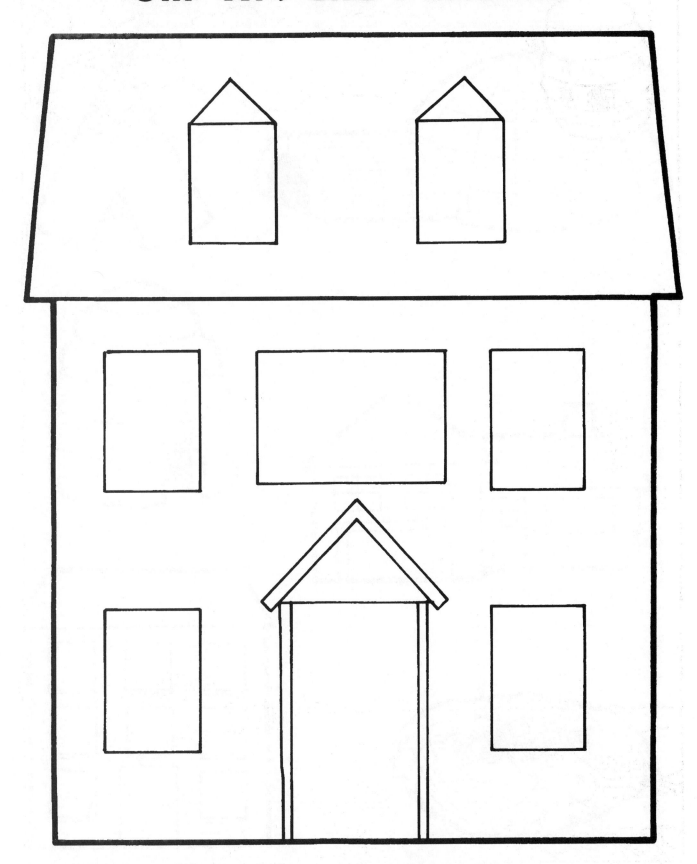

Clip Art and Patterns *(cont.)*

Bookmarks and Badges

Home
is where the
heart is.

I know
the letter
L.

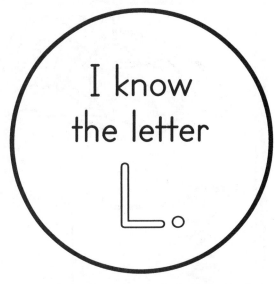

Have students color the hearts and wear their badges home.

Have students color their badges and wear them home.

My
home is

_____.

Help each student fill in the correct color word to describe his or her home. Then have students color their badges to match the colors of their homes. They can wear their badges home.

Although most early childhood students have not yet learned to read, they enjoy having bookmarks to use while reading with their families at home.

Let's read
about homes.

Home Sweet
Home.

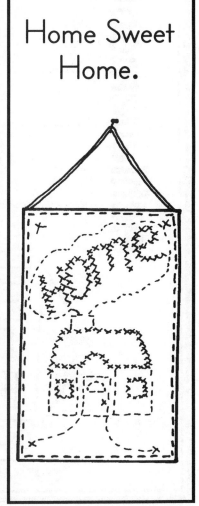

Achievement Award

_____
has earned our
Classroom Achievement Award
for

BEING
A GOOD FRIEND!

_____
Teacher's Signature

_____
Date

Activity (circle time, playtime, etc.)	Monday	Tuesday	Wednesday	Thursday	Friday

Parent Sign In/Out Sheet

Parents: Please sign your child in and out under the current date.

Name	Time	Date:	Date:	Date:	Date:	Date:
	In					
	Out					
	In					
	Out					
	In					
	Out					
	In					
	Out					
	In					
	Out					
	In					
	Out					
	In					
	Out					
	In					
	Out					
	In					
	Out					
	In					
	Out					

Hats and Mittens Activities for Home

Dear Parents and Guardians,

Our theme of the week is hats and mittens. Below is a list of enjoyable activities that you can do with your child. Please use some or all of these activities to support your child's learning. Your help is greatly appreciated.

Suggested Activities:

- If there happens to be a day of snow or chilly weather, put on your winter clothes, including *hats* and *mittens,* and go for a walk together.

- Count all the hats and mittens you have in your home.

- Take your child to the public library. Check out a storybook or nonfiction book that features hats, mittens, and other winter clothes, such as Ezra Jack Keats' *The Snowy Day* (Viking, 1962). Read it together. Discuss your favorite parts with one another.

- Together, imagine that you are a pair of mittens. What do you and your child imagine that mittens might think about all day? What do mittens like to do? Do the same for winter hats.

- Each of you can draw and color a picture of yourself wearing a winter hat and mittens. Tell about your pictures.

- Together with your child, place some winter clothes in a box. Ask your child the purpose of each piece of clothing.

- If your child has a special doll or stuffed toy, make a hat and mittens for it from fabric scraps.

- Read "What Can You Do with a Mitten?" with your child. Ask your child what else you can do with mittens.

Best wishes,

_____

Hats and Mittens Arts and Crafts I

Reproduce the pattern below, making four per student. Have students color, cut, and stitch together a pair of mittens, following the basic directions shown on page 14. Instead of stuffing the mittens, leave the bottoms open and allow students to wear them.

Hats and Mittens Arts and Crafts II

Materials:

- old winter hats
- glue
- buttons, beads, sequins, pompons, rickrack, fabric scraps, etc.
- needles and thread (optional)

Directions:

1. You can send notes to parents on the hats and mittens stationery (page 57), asking them to send old winter hats that they no longer need. If parents do not have enough old hats, purchase some at a local thrift store or cut off the toes of old, clean socks and have students use them as doll hats.

2. Provide students with hats, glue, and a variety of materials for decorating the hat. If you have a number of parent volunteers to help with this activity, you may wish to let students try using needles and thread.

3. Invite each student to decorate a winter hat in any way desired. Allow the glue to dry.

4. Students can wear the hats and mittens (page 46) around the classroom.

Hats and Mittens Story

There are many children's books that deal with winter and winter clothes, so it is likely that your students have already been exposed to several. In this activity, you will work with students to write your own mittens book.

Materials:

- butcher paper and a marking pen or the chalkboard and chalk
- two pieces of laminated construction paper, red and green
- stapler or hole puncher and metal rings
- glue
- strips of writing paper
- drawing paper
- crayons

Directions:

1. Have students sit in a circle. Explain to them that they will be telling a story about a mitten, one idea at a time. Each student, in turn, will add a sentence to the story.

2. Begin the story with the sentence, "Once upon a time, there was a mitten."

3. Write the above sentence and all students' sentences on the chalkboard or butcher paper. If possible, have a classroom helper write each student's sentence on a strip of writing paper, noting on the back the name of the student who suggested it. If no helper is available, you will have to do that yourself in order to complete Step 5.

4. When the story is complete, read it back to students.

5. Glue the strip of writing paper belonging to each student onto the bottom of a piece of drawing paper. Ask each student to illustrate his or her sentence. (You can make a mitten-shaped book by using the pattern on page 46.)

6. After the pictures have been completed, put them together to create a book. Make a construction paper cover with a story title that the class chooses. Use a stapler or a hole puncher and metal rings to fasten the book. List every student's name on the cover or on a title page.

7. Display the book for students and their parents to see or allow students to show it at Open House, Back-to-School Night, or an end-of-the-year party.

Hats and Mittens Letters

Practice the letter **W** for *warm* and *winter.* Tell students that hats and mittens keep us warm during the winter months. Have students color in the giant letters on this page. Ask them to draw and color something else on the back of this page that keeps us warm in the winter.

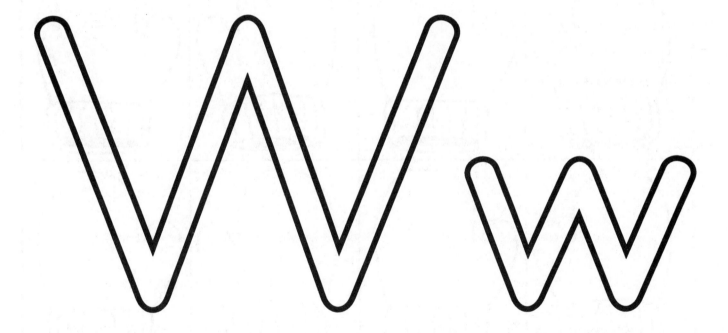

A reward badge for this activity can be found on page 60.

Hats and Mittens Numbers

Send notes to parents on the hats and mittens stationery (page 57) asking them to send to school pairs of mittens and winter hats. Have them label these items clearly so that they can be returned at the end of the day.

As a class, make sets, using the different mittens and hats. You can make sets according to color, size, patterns, or anything else that is easily apparent to students. Together, count the number of items in each set. Ask students to identify the largest and the smallest sets. Then encourage them to identify sets that are of the equal size.

Reproduce the mitten patterns shown below. For individual counting practice, give each student a set of mittens. You may wish to have students color a certain number of mittens on the page or in each row, or you can cut out the mittens and have students count out different sets.

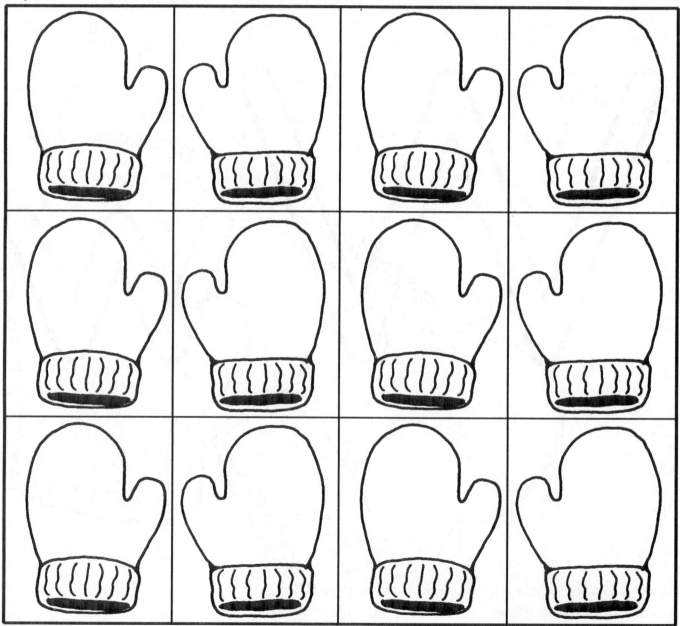

Hats and Mittens Colors

Give each student a set of the patterns shown below, coloring it the color you designate. Alternatively, you might ask, "Who would like to color the red set?" and so forth. Color suggestions include the following: red, blue, yellow, black, white, green, purple, pink, orange, and brown. Once colored, cut out the hats and mittens and display them in the classroom. Then point to one color set at a time. Ask students to name the color and find other things in the room that are the same color. Do this for each color. You may wish to complete the second part of this activity over a few days. It can be time consuming, and trying to review all the colors in one day may make students restless.

A reward badge for this activity can be found on page 60.

Hats and Mittens Shapes

Using the beginning shape of a triangle, each student can make a long winter hat. Trace the triangle onto a large sheet of paper for each student. Ask students to name the shape. Then ask them to color their triangles, making them look like winter hats. You may wish to show students the illustration on this page or present some samples of real long winter hats.

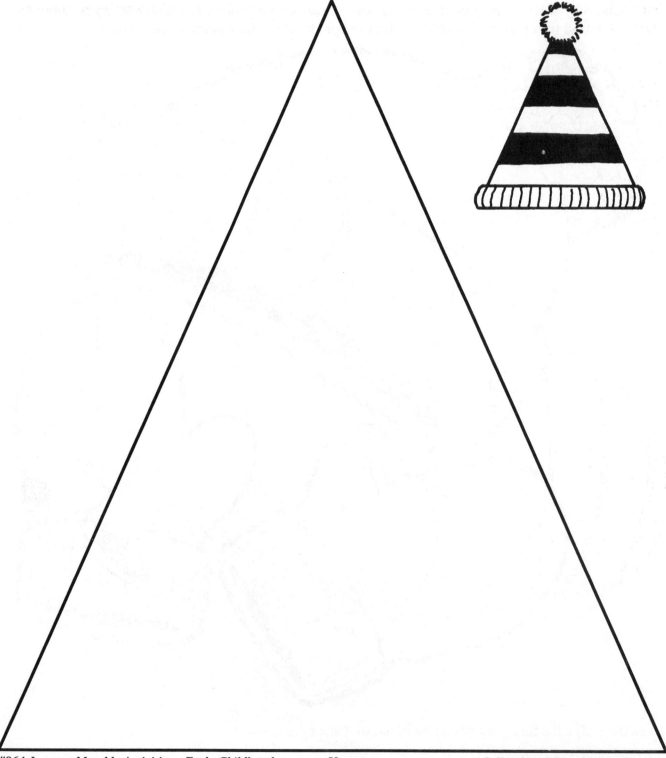

Hats and Mittens Movements

Tell the following story to your students or read aloud Jan Brett's *The Mitten* (Putnam, 1989). Afterwards, ask them if they can name the animals who snuggled inside the mitten. Then have them pantomime the movements of each animal. Retell the story, having students pantomime it as you speak. When you are finished, have them snuggle down for their winter naps!

There is an old folk tale that tells of a young boy who goes out during the winter wearing his mittens. While collecting sticks and twigs to bring home for winter fuel, he loses one of his mittens. Not noticing it is gone, he returns home without it. Meanwhile, a small mouse finds the mitten and snuggles inside to keep warm. A frog passes by and asks if he can also come inside. The mouse agrees. Then comes an owl followed by a rabbit. They ask to enter, and the mouse welcomes them. Next, however, comes a squirrel who pushes in without permission. He is followed by a fox, a deer, and, finally, a bear. The poor mitten is bursting at the seams! It certainly cannot hold another animal, no matter how small. So it is no surprise that when a tiny cricket comes along and sticks in one leg, the mitten tears apart and is left in tatters. The animals scurry in all directions. Just then, the boy returns to find his mitten. Instead, he finds nothing but bits of yarn. Saddened, he walks back home. However, when he returns he is overjoyed to discover that his mother has knitted a new pair of mittens for him while he was gone!

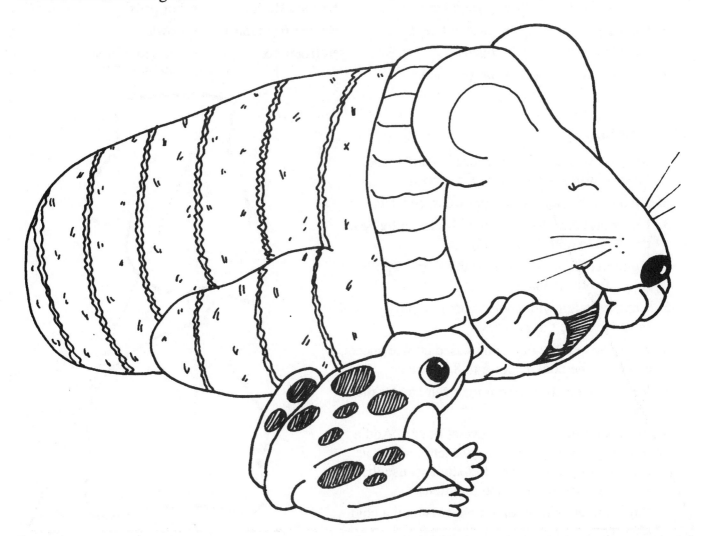

Hats and Mittens Food

Let students make and decorate sugar cookies in the shapes of winter hats and mittens. Create cookie cutters by tracing the patterns shown below onto cardboard and cutting them out. Lay the patterns on top of the dough and cut around them with a plastic knife. The following recipe yields about four dozen cookies.

Note: Ask parents if their children have any food allergies or dietary restrictions.

Ingredients:

- 1 cup (250 mL) sugar
- 2 eggs
- 1 teaspoon (5 mL) baking powder
- 1 teaspoon (5 mL) salt
- food coloring
- ³/₄ cup (185 mL) shortening (part butter, if desired)
- 1 teaspoon (5 mL) vanilla
- 2¹/₂ cups (625 mL) all-purpose flour, plus additional flour
- prepared white frosting

Materials:

- mixing bowl
- rolling pin
- spatula
- dull plastic knives
- plastic wrap
- cutting board
- oven
- large spoon
- cookie sheets
- beater (optional)
- refrigerator
- hot pads
- bowls
- hat and mitten cookie cutter

Preparation:

1. Mix the shortening, sugar, eggs, vanilla, and food coloring (4 to 6 drops) in a bowl.
2. Blend in the flour, baking powder, and salt.
3. Cover and chill for one hour. Meanwhile, heat the oven to 400° F (200° C).
4. Roll the dough ¹/₈" (0.3 cm) thick on a lightly floured cutting board.
5. Cut the dough with cookie cutters lightly dipped in flour or use the patterns.
6. Place the cut dough on ungreased cookie sheets, and bake the cookies for 6 to 8 minutes.
7. Remove the cookies from the oven and let them cool.
8. Place a bit of frosting in several bowls. Add a few drops of food coloring to each, making as many colors as you can. Let students use the knives to frost their hats and mittens.
9. Enjoy the cookies with hot chocolate on a cold afternoon.

Matching Mittens

Draw lines to match each pair of mittens. Color the mittens. Use the same color for each pair.

Challenge: Can you draw a matching hat for one pair of mittens?

What Can You Do With a Mitten?

What can you do with a mitten?
Oh, there are many things!
You can use it in your garden,
Or you can make some wings.
You can dust the chairs and tables,
Or you can mop the floor.
You can make a funny puppet
Or hang it on the door.
You can use it as a washcloth
Or for your dolly's hat.
You can hang it on a flagpole
Or give it to your cat.
You can use it in the bird cage
Or for your ears of corn.
You can put it with your treasures,
And, oh! — It keeps you warm!

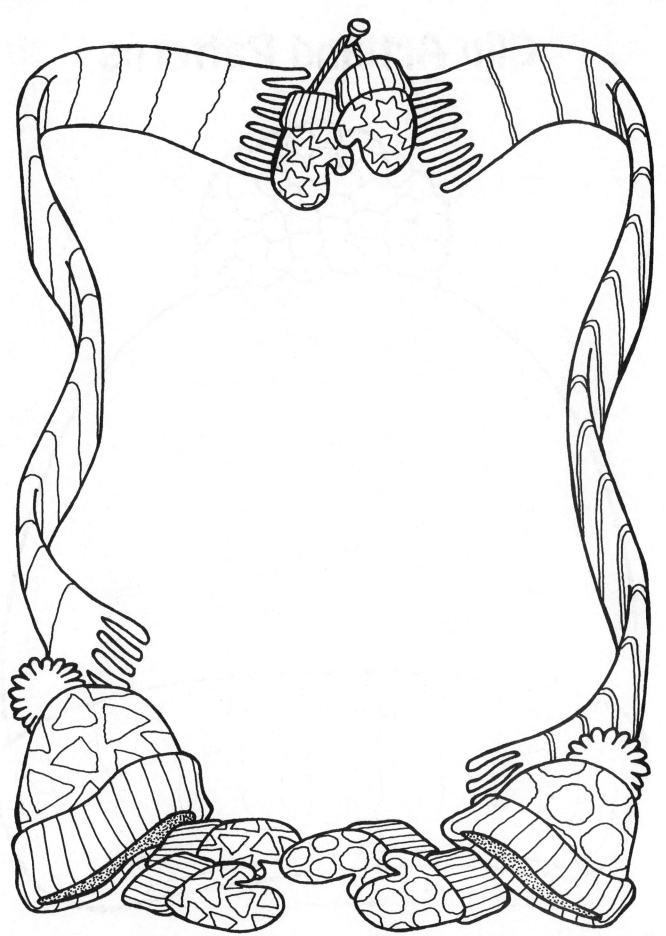

Clip Art and Patterns

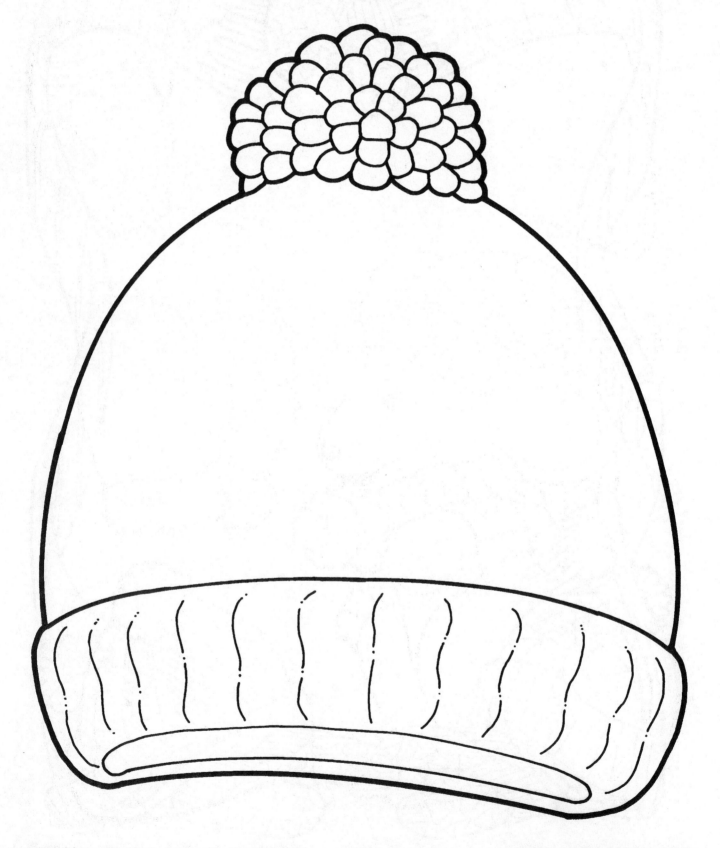

Clip Art and Patterns *(cont.)*

Bookmarks and Badges

I know
the color
_____.

I know
the letter
W.

Fill in each student's color from the activity on page 51. Let each student color the mittens, using that color. Students can wear their badges home.

Have students color their badges and wear them home.

I love
winter!

Let's read
about hats
and mittens.

Keep warm
with a good
book!

Have students color their badges and wear them home.

Although most early childhood students have not yet learned to read, they enjoy having bookmarks to use while reading with their families at home.

Achievement Award

has earned our

Classroom Achievement Award

for

POSITIVE BEHAVIOR!

Date

Teacher's Signature

Activity (circle time, playtime, etc.)	Monday	Tuesday	Wednesday	Thursday	Friday

Parent Sign In/Out Sheet

Parents: Please sign your child in and
out under the current date.

Name	Time	Date:	Date:	Date:	Date:	Date:
	In					
	Out					
	In					
	Out					
	In					
	Out					
	In					
	Out					
	In					
	Out					
	In					
	Out					
	In					
	Out					
	In					
	Out					
	In					
	Out					
	In					
	Out					

Bear Activities for Home

Dear Parents and Guardians,

Our theme of the week is *bears*. Below is a list of enjoyable activities that you can do with your child. Please use some or all of these activities to support your child's learning. Your help is greatly appreciated.

Suggested Activities:

- Pretend that you are a bear family. Imagine the things bears might do as they go through a day. Then pantomime those things.

- For a twist on the above, imagine that though you are all still yourselves, you have bear bodies. Have fun discussing how the changes in eating, sleeping, communicating, touching, and so forth, would make your lives different.

- Take your child to the public library. Check out a bear storybook or nonfiction book. Read it together. Discuss your favorite parts with one another.

- Each of you can draw and color a picture of a bear or a scene with bears. Tell about your pictures.

- Practice growling like a bear.

- If you ever saw a real bear in the wild, tell your child about the experience. If your child has seen one, remind him or her of it and discuss the encounter.

- Visit a toy store to look at some of the stuffed bears there. Ask your child how they differ from real bears.

- Count how many stuffed bears you have in your home.

- Together, watch a bear video or show for children, such as Maurice Sendak's *Little Bear* on the Nickelodeon cable station. You might also watch a nature video of bears or an animated video with realistic bears, such as Walt Disney's *The Fox and the Hound* (1994) or *The Bear* (RCA Columbia Pictures Home Video, 1990). After viewing the video or show, discuss it. Each of you can tell about your favorite parts.

- Read "Little Bear" with your child. Discuss how "Little Bear" is a nickname that a parent might call a child. Ask your child what nicknames he or she is called. If other family members have nicknames, ask your child about those as well.

Best wishes,

_____

Bear Arts and Crafts I

Use the following directions to make a giant bear cave.

Materials:

- large appliance box
- duct tape
- gray paint
- paintbrushes
- old newspapers

- several smaller appliance boxes
- craft knife (for adult use only)
- Styrofoam bowls
- smocks (one per student)
- paints, a variety of colors (optional)

Directions:

1. Inform parents ahead of time of the date for this project since it will be a messy day. You can send notes to parents on the bears stationery (page 76), asking them to send old shirts or smocks if you do not already have some.

2. Ahead of time, build a mock cave from the boxes. Use the large box as the main portion of the cave and the smaller boxes for alcoves and tunnels. Use the craft knife and duct tape to connect the boxes to each other. **Warning:** Students should never use the craft knife. Be sure they remain at a safe distance when you are using it.

3. After the cave has been constructed, lay down old newspapers to cover the classroom floor under and around the boxes. Pour gray paint into the Styrofoam bowls. Give each student a smock, a paintbrush, and some gray paint. Let them paint the entire structure, inside and out, except for the cave floor and underside. These can stay brown like dirt.

4. Let the gray paint dry. If desired, provide different colored paints and allow students to add special gems and minerals or cave paintings to the cave walls.

5. Use this cave for your little classroom bears to hibernate. They can wear bear costumes by completing the activity on page 66.

Bear Arts and Crafts II

Let students become little bears by making the costumes described below.

Materials:

- brown or black construction paper
- patterns (page 67)
- scissors
- tape, glue, or stapler
- safety pins
- brown or black face paint (optional)

Directions:

1. Prepare ahead of time or have students prepare the pattern pieces shown on the next page. Each student will need two ears, one tail, two paw tops, and two paw bottoms cut from brown or black construction paper. Each student will also need a strip of brown or black construction paper that is about 1½" (3.75 cm) wide and 2' (60 cm) long.

2. Glue, tape, or staple the two ears to the front of the strip. Measure and staple each strip to fit around a student's head. Then students can wear their bear ears.

3. Tell students to place the top and bottom of each paw together. Let them use glue or tape around the edges of the front and sides to attach the tops and bottoms. Help students draw on claws and pads as shown on the patterns. They can wear the paws like thumbless mittens.

4. Safety-pin the tail to the back of each shirt or dress.

5. If desired, color students' noses brown or black with face paint.

6. Invite students to growl, waddle, and run like bears. Let them explore their cave (page 65) as well. Have a bear parade around the classroom!

Bear Arts and Crafts II *(cont.)*

tail
(make 1)

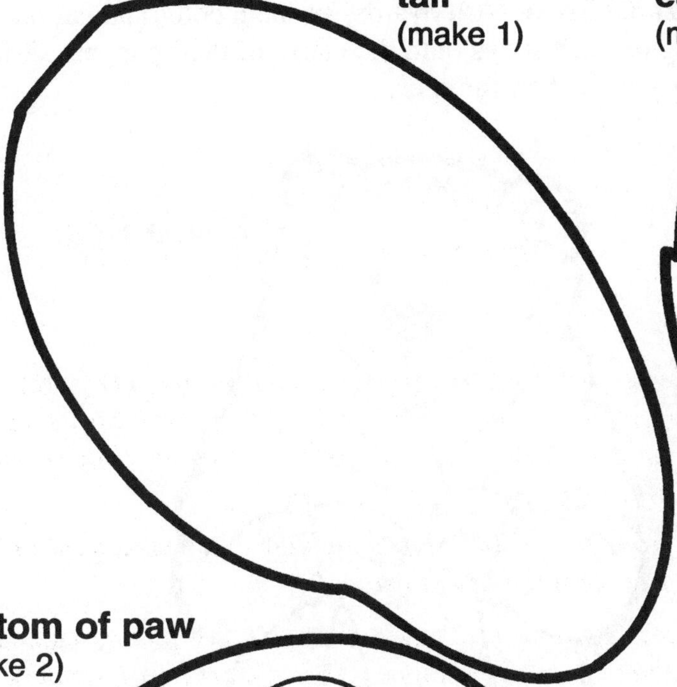

ears
(make 2)

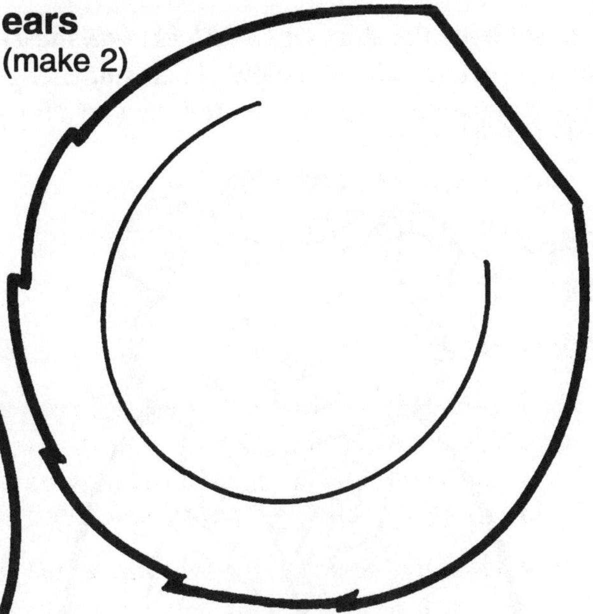

bottom of paw
(make 2)

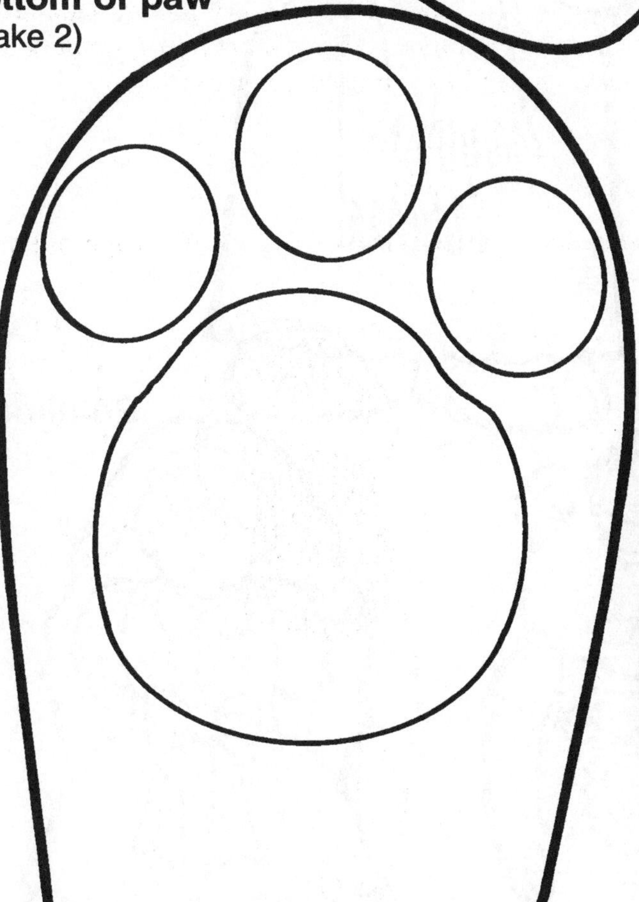

top of paw
(make 2)

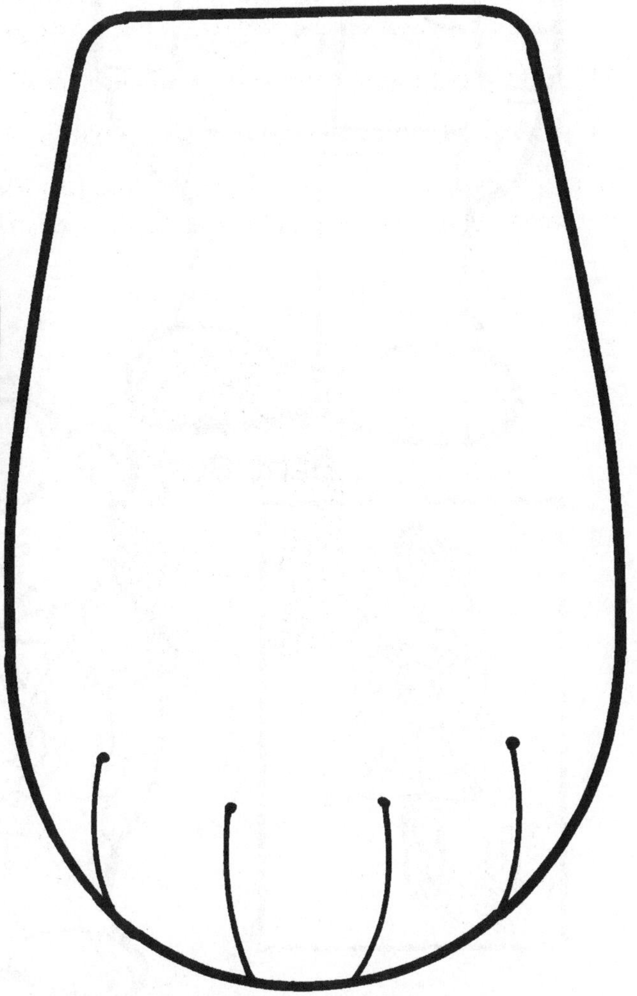

Bear Story

Tell students the story of *Goldilocks and the Three Bears*. Afterwards, let them color and cut out the puppet patterns shown below. Help students glue craft sticks onto the backs of their puppets. Then they can use the puppets to retell the story for you or their families.

Papa Bear

Mama Bear

Goldilocks

Baby Bear

Bear Letters

Practice the letter **B** for *bear*. Have students color in the giant letters on this page. Ask them if they can make the B's look like bears. To do so, they can add lines and details of their own.

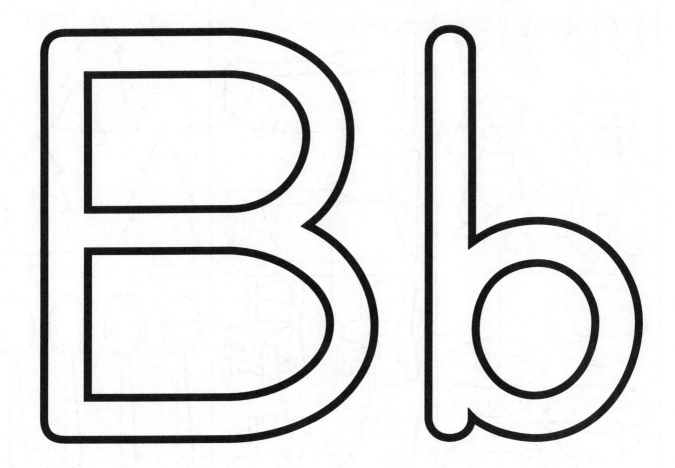

A reward badge for this activity can be found on page 79.

Bear Numbers

After telling the story of *Goldilocks and the Three Bears* (page 68), have students color three of each set shown below. In addition, have them identify sets of three in the classroom and on the playground.

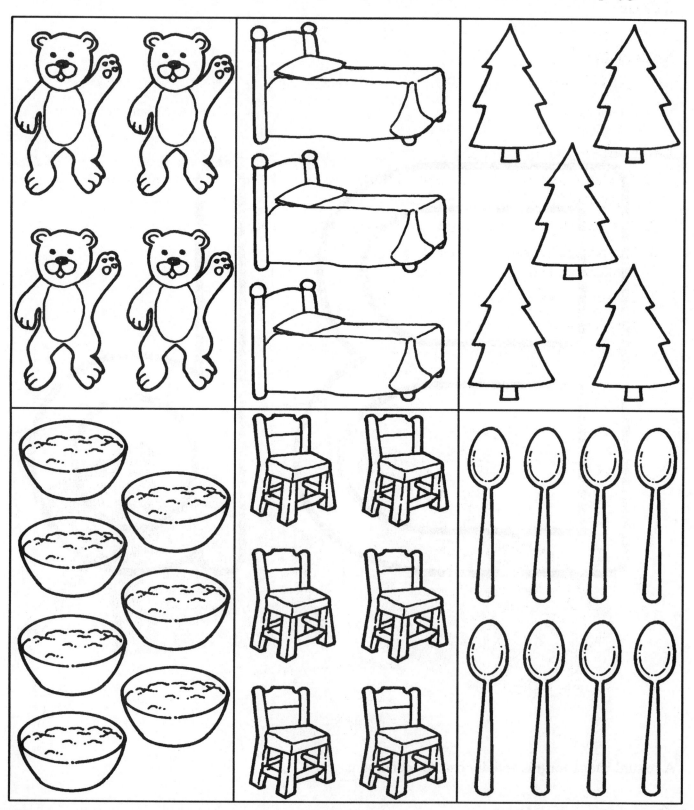

Bear Colors

Bears come in a variety of colors, including black, gray, white, and different shades of these. However, most commonly we think of bears as brown. To learn more about the color brown, engage students in the following activity.

Materials:

- white paper or bear pattern (page 77, one per student)
- brown paint
- large brown pompons
- black markers or crayons

Directions:

1. Give each student a sheet of paper or the bear pattern, brown paint, and a pompon. Tell students to pretend the pompons are fluffy bear tails.

2. Ask each student to paint a picture of a bear, using the pompon as a paintbrush.

3. When the paint is dry, let students use black markers or crayons to add details, such as eyes, noses, and mouths.

4. Let students name their bears.

5. Display the bear paintings.

6. A reward badge for this activity can be found on page 79.

Bear Shapes

Ask students to identify the shapes below. Then give each student a set of the shapes, a separate sheet of paper, glue, and crayons. Show them how to create a bear from these shapes. They can glue the pieces in place and then color in facial features.

Bear Food

Read aloud *Winnie The Pooh* by A. A. Milne (Dutton, 1954). Point out how all bears, including Pooh, like honey. Make this delicious honey treat for your classroom full of hungry little bears.

Note: Ask parents if their children have any food allergies or dietary restrictions.

Ingredients:

- wheat bread
- honey
- peanut butter

Materials:

- knife
- rolling pin
- cutting board
- toothpicks

Preparation:

1. Cut the crust off of several pieces of bread.

2. Use the rolling pin to flatten the bread on the cutting board.

3. Spread a very thin layer of peanut butter on each piece of bread.

4. Spread a very thin layer of honey over the peanut butter.

5. Roll each piece of bread into a tube.

6. Insert toothpicks into the rolled pieces of bread to keep them in place. Position the toothpicks about 1" (2.5 cm) apart.

7. Cut each rolled piece of bread into sections, leaving a toothpick inserted in each.

8. Let your little bears enjoy their honey rolls.

Warning: Tell students to take the toothpicks out of the rolls before eating them. You may wish to add some nuts and berries on the side to make it a real bear treat!

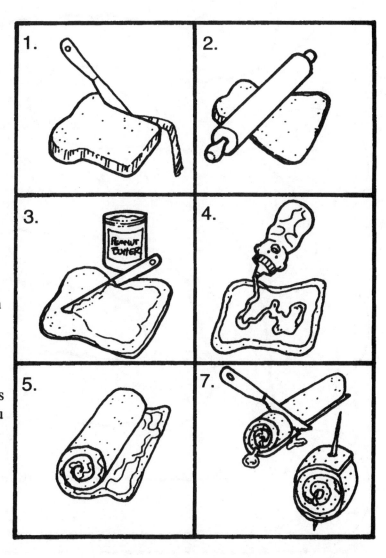

Hibernation

This bear is tired and wants to sleep. Help the bear find its winter cave.

Good Morning, Little Bear!

Good morning, Little Bear!
Good morning, little one!
The nighttime is over.
The morning has begun.

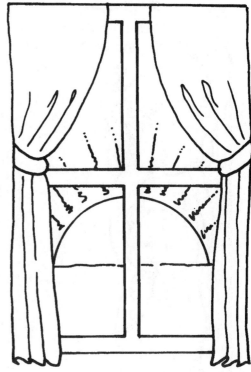

I see you in your cozy bed,
Your rosy nosy peaking out.

Your eyelids flutter open now.
It's time to run and play and
  shout.
Come outside, Little Bear!
Come outside, little one!
The sunshine's calling you.
The daytime has begun.

I see you in your play yard,
A bright twinkle in your eye.
A smile grows upon your face.
As you watch the sun pass by.

Clip Art and Patterns

Clip Art and Patterns *(cont.)*

Bookmarks and Badges

Ask me about a bear named _____.

Write in the name of each student's bear. Let students color their badges and wear them home.

I know the letter **B.**

Have students color their badges and wear them home.

I know the color brown.

Have students color the crayon brown and wear their badges home.

Although most early childhood students have not yet learned to read, they enjoy having bookmarks to use while reading with their families at home.

Let's read about bears.

I'm reading a *beary* good book.

Achievement Award

has earned our

Classroom Achievement Award

for

EXCELLENT LISTENING SKILLS!

_____
Teacher's Signature

_____
Date

80